I0079250

STORYTELLING:
Beyond the Sermon

Preparing to Tell the Ultimate Story

Copyright 2009 Elizabeth A. Perry
All rights reserved.

ISBN # 978-0-578-00831-8

Acknowledgements

Thank you...
to all the storytellers in my life
and to all those who have allowed me
to tell their stories.

Contents

Introduction

Who I am to tell you how to tell stories?

I come from a family of storytellers. Sit two or three of us in a room together and listen to the stories fly! New stories – my parent's latest doctor's appointment, my husband's last audition, my recent trustees meeting – or old stories – Dad's run in with the driver of a segregated bus, Mom's relationships with her co-workers, my siblings' escapades, my children's births – all are shared.

Some people talk in dialog (she said... he said... she said...), others in straightforward facts (the doctor said my tests results are normal), others in extended monologues that struggle to notice others in the room. We talk in stories. Like that Star Trek: The Next Generation episode: *Darmok.*

The Next Generation crew connects with the crew of an alien spaceship. The universal translator doesn't help them understand each other: the words are translated but they don't seem to make any sense. Frustrations abound – and violence – before the captain realizes that his counterpart is speaking in metaphor, telling stories of the past to reflect the situation of the present.

Probably no one in my family thinks of our storytelling as anything unusual; we've talked that way as long as we can remember. It's as normal as drinking iced tea with mint or eating Mom's French Cookies at Christmas. And yet somehow I always knew that it was not innocuous. There was a power held in the telling of stories. Even if I couldn't have articulated the uniqueness of family communication through stories, I did know that it mattered.

When I entered seminary in 1991, post-modernity was on every professor's lips. Some hated the very word, some denied such a thing existed, others were keen students of the philosophy. At least the basic premises of post-modernity were woven into almost every class. Phrases like, "there's no one right way" (to interpret a text, for example) came out of most professors' mouths at least once in the three years I was there. And, whether they named it post-modernity or not, most professors bemoaned the alienation of our era.

In the midst of that, I was blessed to have a few professors who focused on literature, poetry, and stories. I found books by authors unknown to me before... Fish and Ong are two names that stay rooted in my memory because of a single idea I connect with them: that words have substance, that sound fills the space between speaker and listener. Those and others like them helped me to find words for the power I had always known existed in stories.

The storytelling that had been a part of me, became also a part of the way I saw the world, the Creator of the world, and the relationships between us all.

From then till now, I have been an avid student of the story and the power of storytelling – too teach, learn, identify, relate, unite, divide, heal, disrupt, and transform. I believe that power is why Jesus used stories so often and I believe that the power of the story is just as available to us today. We can use stories, use the power of storytelling, to prepare to do the work the Ultimate Storyteller has laid out for us to do: sharing the Ultimate Story with the world.

Theories of Stories and Storytelling

Telling stories requires effort but, when done well, it results in the power to form identity, to teach, to entertain, to sell, to reveal or manipulate the truth, and to subvert or repress.

Chapter 1: Power

Storytelling is not child's play. It requires preparation and practice; it has power.

Several years ago, I was the opening luncheon speaker for the Pennsylvania Pastors Conference. The theme was Judaism, Christianity, and Islam; I was asked to do something interactive with about 400 people.

I decided to retell the biblical story of Abraham, Sarah, Hagar, Isaac, and Ishmael – and then to add to that the story of Mohammad and some of the creation stories of Islam. All of it was to be told around the theme of following God.

The basic story was there for me in the Bible – I wrote an outline starting with Abram and Sarai's departure from Ur. I chose phrases straight from the scripture so that it would sound familiar to the pastors in the audience. Then I checked several reference books on Islam and noted where the stories diverged. I continued through the death of Abraham, his burial by both his sons, and the list of descendents of Isaac and Ishmael. Then I added some of the history about Mohammad and his followers and the beliefs of Islam.

The outline of the talk took me several weeks to put together. After that came the months of editing, which continued until almost the day of the luncheon! I wanted to be able to speak the story rather than read it, so everything I wrote had to sound exactly the way I speak, while keeping those important biblical phrases.

Once I had the story finished, I began to work on making it interactive. I decided that I would stop the story from time to time and ask the audience questions that would connect them with the characters in the story, and with each other. I planned those questions as carefully as I'd plotted the story.

In a post-911 world, I was asking Christian clergy to connect with a story of Jews, Christians, and Muslims. I was asking them to acknowledge aloud, in the midst of other Christian clergy, that their lives and the lives of Jews and Muslims had similarities. I was asking them to see more of the relationship in scripture than they had done before. And I was asking them to agree that not only did we all worship the same God and come from the same ancestors, we all had at times lost our path as we attempted to follow God.

I knew those were huge leaps that had to be accomplished one step at a time. So I planned the questions so that the answers could move from very short responses around the whole table to longer responses between two or three people.

For example, the first question (as Sarai and Abram moved from Ur to Haran and on again) was, "How many times have you moved?" The attendees had thirty seconds to respond, going around the table saying only their names and the number. Later questions were more probing: as Sarah and Abraham longed for a child, "Have you ever wanted something beyond the bounds of common sense?"

The responses were fascinating. At first the room was relatively quiet but as the questions went on, people were easier with each other, noisier, laughing and sharing openly. But as the questions became more intimate and serious, the room became quieter, the voices lower, the sharing more intense.

By the end of the luncheon, I felt sure the talk had been a success. There were, however, ramifications I hadn't expected.

The first was this: what they learned from me in the story laid the groundwork for everything else they learned during the Conference. People told me that if they hadn't been at the luncheon they wouldn't have understood some of the other speakers. I think we can call that the content power – if I hadn't done my homework on the basic story, if I had gotten the facts wrong or misinformed them in some way, my story could have undermined everything the Conference was about!

The second was this – perhaps we can call it the context power. Not only did the story, the questions, and the answers connect the pastors to the story and to each other, it connected them to me in ways I had not anticipated.

One man waited for me outside the door of the following sessions; one woman followed me everywhere, even into the bathroom! Because I had been telling the story, they connected me to their conversations with each other. They made assumptions about me based on their insights, learning, and relationships. While I told them little about myself in the process, they filled in the gaps with their own understandings and opinions. And the result was not comfortable for me or for them as I had to correct their mistakes.

I believe this experience points out two important facts about stories.

First, stories take a lot of work. If you are going to tell a major story in a major event, plan on months of preparation time. Even if it is a short story in a small setting, give yourself weeks to work on it and make sure it is all that it needs to be. (See the end of this book for practical ways of honing your storytelling skill.)

Second, more importantly, stories have incredible power. Be prepared, as best you can, for the outcome of the storytelling, and be as responsible as you can in the use of that power. The next several chapters will deal with those power issues in more depth.

Questions –

1. Have you ever told a story without enough preparation? What was the result for you? For your audience?

2. Have you ever had a story be more or less successful than you expected? How did you handle that?

3. Have you ever had an unexpected outcome to a story you've told. Was there a way you could have prepared for that?

Chapter 2: Identity

Storytelling has the power to shape identity.

When I was a child, my grandmother told me a story about her father. In a storytelling family, this shouldn't be unusual but the content of this story and the way she told it remained with me. It is one of the factors that shaped my identity.

When Grandma was a little girl, she, her parents, and her nine siblings lived along the Pennsylvania Canal. Barges moved along the Canal, transporting passengers and products, pulled by mules who walked along paths on either side of the Canal. The paths were also easy walkways for people who couldn't afford to ride on the barges.

Hoboes walked the Canal paths regularly. Hoboes were unemployed homeless men who went from one community to another looking for work, shelter, and food. Grandma explained that hoboes would knock on the door of the houses along the Canal, asking for help. If they weren't sent on their way, they'd be invited to the kitchen door and given a sandwich to eat while sitting on the back steps. As they left, they'd draw a symbol on the house with a piece of chalk – so the next hobo who came by would know this was a good place to stop. And as soon as they were out of sight, the owner came out to wash off the mark!

Except my great-grandfather, Grandma said frostily. No matter how little food they had, he always invited the hoboes into the house. They always sat with the family and shared equally in the food.

And, she said with both amazement and disdain, as if all the years still hadn't erased the memory of her own hunger, "He never washed the mark off the porch!"

Even as a young child, I was in awe of that story. It explained to me so many things about my family. It explained why when Grandma cut a slice of pie at Thanksgiving, it was one-quarter of the pie! It explained why when someone gave her two half-gallons of ice cream every week, she passed one on to us. It explained why no one wandered through our yard without being invited onto the porch for a glass of iced tea or a freshly-baked whoopee pie.

That was our identity: we were a family who fed people. While Grandma implied that her father was wrong, she continued what he had taught her, and passed it down to me, both in story and in actions, and I continued the tradition in my family and in my work. It is part of who I am, as a pastor and as a person: I feed people, spiritually and physically. I can't think of a better identity to have learned, a better story to have heard.

You can see that same identity shaping going on in the stories Jesus told. The Good Samaritan, the Prodigal Son – stories designed to give his audience role models. Those stories said, "Here is an identity worth having – shape your life around it!"

When you tell your stories, recognize that they can shape the identity of your audience.

Questions –

1. Is there a story that has shaped your identity? How would you tell that story?

2. Is there a story that reflects who you are now? Is it a story you would be comfortable telling someone else?

3. Is there a story you would like to see shape your identity? How could you tell yourself that story?

Chapter 3: Teaching

Storytelling has the power to teach.

I studied French for three years during high school. I hated almost every minute of it. I made fun of the teacher, I acted out, I avoided my homework. Probably, I know now, because I just don't have an ear for languages.

Perhaps because of that general lack, or because of all the homework I didn't do, I don't know much French today. I can say, "Je ne parle pas francais." (I don't speak French.) And "Regardez le neige." (Look at the snow.) And "Ou est le bureau de tabac." (Where is the tobacco shop?)

The one thing that I did learn in French class was the story of Edit Piaf. The teacher brought in a phonograph and an LP (yes, it was that long ago...) and played her songs for us. We learned one of those songs and I still remember it today. "No, rein de rein. No je ne regret rein. Ni la bien que ma fait, ni la mal, tu c'est mais bien egal." (No, nothing at all. No, I regret nothing. Neither the good, nor the bad, its all equal.)

Edit had a difficult life and yet she could look back on it regretting nothing either good or bad because it had all been equally a part of her life. I'm not sure why that struck me so strongly in high school, when my life had been to that point so easy. But it came back to me many times as the years got harder. Don't regret anything because it all makes you who you are.

I learned more French from a song than from three years of studying. And I learned a moral lesson from the story of that singer.

Think about the fairy tales and stories of your childhood: what did they teach you? Morals, ethical codes, acceptable behaviors and beliefs were all woven into the stories each generation has learned. Little Red Riding Hood taught young girls not to venture out alone; The Little Engine that Could taught little boys to keep trying; Things that Go Bump in the Night taught children not to be afraid of the unknown.

Jesus' stories used the same power: David eating the sacred bread taught his audience that it was acceptable for his disciples to pick and eat corn as they walked on the Sabbath; the story of the sower taught them that they could be fertile soil for the seeds of this teaching.

When you tell stories, your audience will learn from them. Make sure that the lessons are worth teaching.

Questions –

1. What stories have you learned from? Start with the cartoons you watched as a child and end with the last theater performance you saw – what did those stories teach you?

2. Who was your favorite teacher? Least favorite? Why? What lessons about storytelling can you learn from them?

3. What do you think will be the most powerful lesson you will teach? Is there a story you can think of that teaches that lesson?

Chapter 4: Entertainment

Storytelling has the power to entertain.

There was a short lived science fiction show on television several years ago, *Firefly,* that became a minor movie, *Serenity*, and the subject of a collection of essays, also titled *Serenity*. In all three media – TV show, movie, and book – it was very entertaining!

The colors, the scenery, the music – all were woven intricately into the fabric of the television show and movie to create a setting uniquely its own. Each character was designed to be multi-faceted, to draw you in, to make you want to know more about them! And the plot of each episode built upon the previous one so you wanted to watch again, you wanted to learn more.

In the book, the essays each told the story of someone's exposure to, interaction with, and thoughts about *Serenity*'s entertainment. Like the show and the movie, the essays had settings, characters, and a plot: as a whole the book shared the movement of a community who formed around their love of the show and grieved its loss.

The use of storytelling in contemporary media is astounding. Music videos added a secondary level of storytelling to the words of songs. Video games that began with getting a frog across a road now take their characters into a virtual world. Websites tell the stories of the lives of individuals in intricate detail – their settings, their character, and the plots that move their days.

These media – physical and electronic – entertain, and entertainment is powerful. Entertainment connects us to our emotions; entertainment allows our guard to be down; entertainment creeps into our subconscious while we aren't even looking.

Entertainment is connected in our conscious minds to childhood and innocence but it has power strong enough to shape societies. When we relax and receive stories as entertainment, they have the power to work below the conscious level and, intentionally or not, to be subversive or repressive, to encourage people to rebellion or conformity.

Uncle Tom's Cabin, for example, influenced the emotions of people in the northern part of the United States and encouraged their outrage against slavery. Those fairy tales mentioned in the last chapter, taught morals, social order, belief systems in Europe. The gospel stories, told and retold by traveling disciples, spread Christian faith long before dogma and doctrine enforced belief.

As you prepare to tell your stories, recognize that people will let their guard down, allow you in to entertain them, and that in doing so they will allow your story to have a great power in their lives.

Questions –

1. What is your favorite form of entertainment? Does it include storytelling in any way?

2. Is it okay to just entertain people with stories? Is the answer to that different if the people are at home? In school? In worship?

3. Why did we stop telling stories in worship for so many years? Do you think entertainment took power away from storytelling?

Chapter 5: Advertising

Storytelling has the power to sell.

When I was about seven, my parents bought their first television. I remember how exciting it was, the set coming into the house, the antenna going up on the roof, the black and white picture that I now know was grainy and blurred. Back then, I thought it was perfect!

I also remember seeing Barbie dolls advertised on that TV. Barbie's clothes, Barbie's car and Barbie's house and Barbie's bed. Barbie's long black sequined dress and tall microphone stand. Barbie's wedding dress and Ken's tuxedo. Barbie's tennis outfit and racquet. The clothing and accessories shown in each advertisement told a story – the story of a teenage girl; a young woman just coming into the fullness of life; a girl who could sing, and love, and play, and work; the woman we all hoped we'd become.

My daughter watched similar ads when she was young – Barbie had by then acquired a yacht and a mansion, more friends, and the ability to change jobs by the hour. The advertising was slicker, more intense and frequent, but the story was the same – Barbie was the young woman who had it all. And children should have all that Barbie has. My daughter wanted it all, too, just as I had. I can't tell you how many times I went into my daughter's room and the entire floor was covered with Barbie dolls and their possessions!

Now, my granddaughter is playing with today's version of those dolls. Barbie as a princess, Barbie as a butterfly, Barbie in High School Musical II. Barbie's internet home page is set up like a house, and the computer on her desk invites us into her world. The wide-screen TV on the opposite wall offers children a chance to see again their favorite commercials.

Barbie isn't the only example of storytelling as a means to sell. A few years ago, Folger's ran a series of ads based on the unfolding of a relationship born around a cup of coffee –Target ran an ad where a couple changed clothes to reflect the story of their lives – Secret had a deodorant ad campaign that exposed family secrets – a facial tissue ad series shared people's tearful admissions.

Stories frequently find their way into advertising. Why? Because stories have the power to sell. A story can make an emotional appeal in a way that a straight-forward list of benefits cannot. A story can give us a frame of reference from our own lives – our childhood dreams for the woman we could become – that will match up with the product we're being sold. We can see ourselves in the story; we can see ourselves with the product.

You may not be in a position of selling toys or clothing or deodorant but you are in a position of selling ideas and beliefs – as well as the charitable organization we call the church. You can use storytelling to help your listeners become more tied into your beliefs and your organization.

Just remember to tell your stories with integrity, without coercion or manipulation, and you'll follow in the footsteps of the greatest of storytelling sellers: Jesus of Nazareth.

Questions –

1. What products can you think of that use stories to sell? Do you like the ads? Why or why not?

2. What are you, as a Christian storyteller, selling? Is it of value to the buyer?

3. Does it bother you to compare spreading the faith to advertising, marketing, or selling? Why or why not?

Chapter 6: Truth

Storytelling has the power to reveal or to manipulate the truth.

My mother told me this story about her mother, her sister, and herself.

Mom and her sister were about four and three, respectively. They lived with their parents, older brother, and younger brother on a farm in York County, Pennsylvania. The family was poor and the work was hard. My grandmother often had to help my grandfather with the farm work as well as doing all the household chores.

So one day, while she was out working on the farm, those two little girls decided they would help out their over-worked and much loved mother. The decided they would wash the wooden kitchen floor!

They poured out a bucket of water across the floor. They found several bars of homemade soap. And they knelt down in the water and began scrubbing. It wasn't long till the scrubbing became sliding and soon they were skating around the kitchen floor with bars of soap on their hands and knees!

Into that mess walked my grandmother! She froze in the doorway for a moment, then dropped what she was carrying, sat down in the midst of the soapy water, and hugged her two sopping wet, sticky daughters. And laughed.

For several years, I told that story to congregations. It was to me a metaphor for how God treats the messes we make in our lives: just sits down with us in the midst of it and gathers us up in God's arms. So one Sunday afternoon, sitting on the porch swing at my mother's home, I told her what I had said that Sunday morning. And I repeated the story she had told me and my point to the congregation.

She didn't say anything and when I looked at her, she had this sheepish sort of smile on her face. "Well," she finally said, "she might have been a little angry."

What is the truth to that story? Which is the true version: the first one my mother told me? Or the postscript she added years later? Who gets to decide?

Who owns this story? Is it my mother's story? Or her mother's – who is gone many years now? Or is it my story about my grandmother and my mother which, like so many others, has helped shape my life?

In some situations, ownership of a story is very easy – whoever holds the copyright. For many stories however, it isn't that easy. There are multiple versions of many folk tales, multiple viewpoints to all family stories. Even the gospels tell differing versions of biblical stories!

How do storytellers make sure they are telling the truth? How can we be honest in the telling? How can we see beyond the entertainment and teaching value of a story to whether it is true or not?

How can we make sure we are not being manipulative in the telling of our stories? For example, my aunt died of cancer in her late 70's. I could tell the story and follow it with, "and that little girl in her mother's arms would later die of cancer." Technically, it would be true and it might be emotionally powerful! But it wouldn't be honest – it wouldn't be storytelling with integrity.

There are no easy answers to these questions of integrity. We as storytellers have to be as searching as we can be, as skeptical as we can be, as deliberately honest as we can be. We have to find out as much background to the stories we tell as possible. Is there an original author to the story? If it is about living people, can we contact them? Is it published somewhere? If there are several versions of the story, which one will we focus on?

Each year in the lectionary, we find stories that will be told again the following year in a slightly different form, with perhaps a slightly different meaning. (Consider the two forms of the Beatitudes, for example.) It is part of our job to help our congregations to see the differences and understand them. Not to confuse them but to help them move, as Paul said, from the milk to the meat.

Let me go back to my mother's story for a moment. Which is the true version of that story about washing the kitchen floor? Well, probably the second one. The first was the idealized remembrance of a woman who loved her mother; the second held a re-awakened memory caused by hearing her own story told by another.

Which bring us to who owns that story? Well, probably my mother: she made that clear when she corrected me on the porch that day. I can't change her story if I want to tell it as truth.

But I also own it too. The first version of the story is one that, along with great-grandfather's hoboes, has shaped who I am. The true story for my life is that once upon a time, my mother told me a story about her childhood that taught me about love and forgiveness. What details she missed in the first telling, did not affect me then.

So what do I do with this story now as a pastor? I tell it as my story: This is what my mother told me and this is what it taught me about love. But I always leave space to tell the second layer of the story and what it taught me about truth. Because that second layer, told on the porch swing that day, is also part of my story and part of who I am.

As you tell your stories, be storytellers of integrity and be careful with the truth.

Questions –

1. Be honest: have you ever told someone else's story as if it happened to you? Have you ever told a story you were sent in an email without checking to see if it was true? Have you ever edited someone's story so that it was more emotive or just fit your purpose better? Did you ever tell a true story without getting permission? Were you speaking with integrity?

2. Imagine you could share a scripture story with one of the characters from it. How would they react? For example, how do you think Judas would react to hearing the story of his betrayal? Martha to hearing the story of her impatience with Mary?

3. Do you know stories you would never repeat? Why wouldn't you tell them?

Chapter 7: Subversion

Storytelling has the power to subvert or repress.

I sat on the cement step at the top of a flight of stairs leading from my parent's back yard to the expanse of lawn that spread to the Susquehanna River. My grandson sat beside me – he was probably about four or five at the time. I was telling him about growing up there. I wanted him to know what his great-grandfather, then in his mid-80's, had been like when I was a child.

When I was a little girl, I was sitting here with mom and dad on a summer day. We were watching the river roll by and enjoying the flowers. Some people were swimming in the river – down there by the bridge. It's dangerous there, the water going around the bridge drags the ground away and makes it very deep and the current is swift. One of the people got in trouble and started shouting, 'Help! Help!" My dad jumped out of his chair, ran down these stairs we're sitting on, ran to the bridge, jumped in the water, and saved that swimmer from drowning!

I wasn't sure how much he understood – he was very young to understand danger and heroism, risk and salvation – but I thought that if he heard the story he might understand his grandfather a little more. And he might remember the story someday when someone would be depending on him.

A few minutes later I left him coloring on the porch as I went inside to talk to the grown-ups. And then we heard him quietly calling in a whisper, "Help... help... help..."

I told my father what I had shared with my grandson and he went out to the porch. The two of them sat in quiet conversation for a long time.

39

It may seem innocuous but I was doing a very dangerous thing, telling that story to such a small child.

Because this was a subversive story. It was a story that said the vision you have now of this old man who loves you but isn't able to play with you or be active with you – this isn't all the truth. It was a story that, I hoped, would teach him to look beyond the obvious for the deeper truth. A truth, in this case, that my father verified when he made the effort to answer his great-grandson's whispered call.

I could have told the story in a repressive way, had I had a different goal in mind. I could have told it in a way that made him afraid of the river, for example. Or afraid of growing old himself. Or any of a dozen other lessons.

I also could have used the story in a way that was manipulative – trying to manufacture emotions in my grandson like fear or envy or pride or even love. But I tried to tell the story in a transformative way – leaving space for my grandson to turn it into his own story. Which he did.

Jesus told subversive, transformative stories that made room for listeners to step inside a different world. When you tell stories remember that they have the power to subvert and repress, to manipulate and to transform. Do the best you can to allow people space to hear your story and make it their own.

Questions –

1. Have you ever heard a story that subverted your worldview or repressed you from making a change? How did it feel? What affect did it have on you?

2. Is there a story that could subvert the way you see the world now? What would it be about?

3. Is there a story that could transform your life? Where can you look for that story?

Elements of Stories

Christian stories are made up of four elements: setting, character, plot, and moral.

Chapter 8: Setting

Setting is the where and when of a story – its location in time and space. It includes places, institutions, eras, and events.

Another of those family stories told over and over again was about my dad and his run-in with a bus driver in the South. Dad had given his seat to an African-American woman and the bus driver refused to move the bus till dad sat back down. Dad threatened the driver and the bus moved on with the woman firmly seated.

In the 1990's I was leading a series of workshops on diversity and wanted to use that story. So I went to my parent's home armed with a tape recorder and asked dad to tell me the story in as much detail as he could. With some questions and prodding, he added a good many details that I hadn't heard before.

Dad was a truck driver at the time, which was about 1940, hauling cars from Detroit around the East Coast. But he also drove military vehicles south, ones too big to fit on a truck, and then rode a train back home to Pennsylvania. He had just delivered such a vehicle and was taking a bus to the train station.

The bus drove through a worn-out area with miles between stops and no houses anywhere within sight. At one stop a very pregnant African-American woman got on the bus. Dad said he couldn't imagine how far she must have walked to get on the bus and he automatically got up to let her sit down.

The bus didn't move. He asked the driver, "What are you waiting for?" And the driver responded, "I'm waiting for you to sit back down!" Dad said, "You'll have a hell of a long wait!" and then, "I can drive the damn bus if I have to!"

The bus moved on.

At some point in my questions, one slipped out that I hadn't actually thought about in advance – "Where was this bus?" – and his answer froze me. "Between Montgomery and Selma."

All my memories of the Civil Rights Movement came flooding back to me and hit me right between the eyes! My father could have been killed that day! If it had been 1960 instead of 1940, my father probably wouldn't have made it back from that trip south!

What had been a good story before – a story about honor and putting person before race – became a heroic story. And all because the setting was suddenly not some anonymous road in the South but the road between Montgomery and Selma. The name of those two towns held a history, had weight and power, created a backdrop for the story, a setting that changed the very meaning of the story for me.

The story of the woman at the well who speaks with Jesus would not have had the same power had the story not been set in Samaria. The settings for our stories tell part of the story. As you plan your storytelling, remember to make sure that you present the setting in a way that supports and empowers your story.

Questions –

1. List all the settings that apply to your life: time, space, era, place, institution, social strata, political system, etc. What do they say about the setting for the story of your life?

2. What is so remarkable about the setting for your favorite book, movie, or theater performance? How does it enhance the point of the story?

3. Should the setting come at the beginning of a story or can it be effective at the end? Or in the middle?

Chapter 9: Character

Characters are the "who" of a story, the animate and/or inanimate objects that populate a story. The characters also might include the speaker and the audience (both the original and the current).

A decade ago, I received a phone call late one night. "Tash died today. We're gathering at Heaven. Would you come over there with us?"

Tash was a young man who had been a friend of my son since high school. Heaven was a restaurant in town. And "we" were the dozens of people he counted as friends. The owner of Heaven was one of those friends and he closed the upper floor restaurant so we could all be together to share the grief. We sat in between the gold pillars with the pale blue walls and puffy white clouds surrounding us and talked about our memories of Tash and how much he was loved.

His friends asked me if I would lead the funeral service – no one knew anything about his family or even if he had any family – and I was honored. A day or so later, an uncle called me and repeated the request. There was extensive family, living in the same city, but they hadn't had any contact with Tash for years.

As I talked with people, I realized what a difficult service this would likely be. Tash had realized he was gay when he was still in high school and his family had kicked him out. He had moved in with friends and never contacted his family again but parts of his heritage had always stayed with him. He became a very popular drag queen, sometimes singing gospel songs and assuring people in the audience of the love of God for them. His family knew nothing of this – as his friends had not known the family even existed.

When we gathered in the funeral home, there weren't enough chairs in the building to hold all the people. People were six deep across the back of the room and the latecomers were standing in the doorway and hall.

The tension between them was so great that I hoped just to get through the service without a fight breaking out. The family resented the presence of friends they felt had taken their child from them; the friends resented the presence of a family they felt had deserted their friend.

They even had different names for him. The friends called him, as I did, Tash – short for Tasha -- and usually referred to Tash as "her." The family called him Bill.

The family brought posters full of pictures of Bill – all as a child of less than twelve. The friends brought long-stemmed red roses.

The service was a conglomeration of "she" and "he", "him" and "her" – a James Weldon Johnson reading called "Go Down, Death" and the scripture story of the death of David's friend Jonathan – the drama of torn black cloth and red roses piled by a child's picture.

Ask anyone at that service who Tash was as a character in his own life story and you'd get a different answer depending on who you talked to. His family knew a different character, known by a different name, than his friends knew. The story told by a cousin, for example, would be totally different than the story told by a roommate. The story told by a co-worker completely different than one told by an aunt.

Not only was Tash a character in his own story, not only did his friends and family people his story – the teller of that story would determine the content and the quality of the story you heard.

While Tash's story is more dramatic than most, it is true of all stories: the characters are not only the animate and inanimate objects in the stories. The characters include also the teller of the story and the audience. They can change the content and the context – and the meaning.

Would Jesus' stories have had the same power if they had been told by someone who was not God incarnate? Would they have the same meaning to us if they had not been first told to those who became the founders of the Christian church?

People your stories with good characters but also remember that you affect the story by who you are. And your audience does the same.

Question –

1. Who is the most important character in the story of your life? You? God? Someone else?

2. Think of a story you have told. How did your understanding of it affect its impact on your audience?

3. Can an audience affect the point of a story? How might you need to adapt a story to fit your audience?

Chapter 10: Plot

Plot is the "what" of a story – the events – and the "how" – the movement of the story from past through present into future. The plot includes tension and resolution.

Several years ago, I performed a wedding for friends – a young couple who had known each other for some time: professionals, well-educated, well-traveled, and multi-cultural. They came from varying backgrounds – Jewish, Catholic, Protestant – and their histories were important to them, as were their friends, their work, and the ways in which they could, individually and as a couple, affect the world.

They wanted their wedding to reflect their commitment to their past, their commitment to each other, and their commitment to the larger world.

We talked about the general components of a wedding service in almost any religious or cultural setting and about the ways in which those components were reflected in different communities of faith.

In that conversation, we came to one image that seemed to pull together all their concerns: the Jewish wedding canopy. That canopy reflects the sky above and the way in which the whole world is reflected in the couple about to marry. It brings to mind the words, "In the beginning..." and sets this couple's marriage in the context of all God's works. I began to see their wedding as the central plot point in a story about their lives and God's work.

The service began:
> Once upon a time, there was no world. No canopy of sky; no platform of earth. Nothing. And then God created, out of that nothing, a world. And filled that world with people.

People created to need each other, to want each other, to fall in love with each other.

Once upon a time, there was no couple before me. No Ted; no Melissa. And then God created them. Out of the people that came before them, falling in love and joining together, these two were born. Out of their individual histories, out of their individual experiences, they were created into the people they are today. And out of that innate need we all have for each other, they -- like generations before -- met and fell in love.

Once upon a time, you and I were strangers. Now we have been brought together to this time and this place to witness their marriage, to stand with them in their commitment to each other, and to bless them along into their future.

The plot of any story is the movement from the past, through the present, and into the future. For Christian stories, the plot has an extra dimension. Christian plots have at their heart a movement toward God. Christian stories tell how people work their way, through tension and resolution, from the people they used to be toward the people God is calling them to be.

The movement may be small, not every story will bring its characters into the fullness of God's intention for them. Some stories may even tell of failures to move into the kindom. But there is an understanding within the storyteller, to be heard by the audience, that this story, each story, tells us something about God and humanity as they struggle to reach each other.

Questions –

1. Naturalists say that there are only a few basic shapes to be found in nature. Is that true of story plots? Are there a few basic plots and all stories just adaptations of them?

2. Can all story plots fit somewhere into the plot of God's salvation of humanity? How would you think about a story's plot in light of the salvation story?

3. If you were called on to tell a story about your movement toward God, what story would you tell?

Chapter 11: Moral

The moral of a story is the "why"- the lesson to be learned from a Christian story. It's the theological, philosophical, and psychological element.

When I taught world religions to undergraduate students, I began every class with a story. Generally, they were folk tales or traditional stories from one of the religions we were studying. Several stories showed up in multiple religions, albeit with different meanings.

One of those was the Christian story of the mustard seed, or as it is known in Buddhism, the story of the grain of rice.

In the Christian story, a woman's son dies and she asks a religious leader to bring him back to life. The leader tells her, "Go find a mustard seed from a house that has never known sorrow. Bring it back to me and I will give you what you seek." She leaves and begins to knock on her neighbors' doors. At each house she hears the same thing: "Of course, we've known sorrow. Let me tell you about it."

The Buddhist version of the story begins similarly. Buddha's sister has a son who dies and she asks him to bring the boy back to life. Buddha tells her to "Go find a grain of rice from a house that has never known sorrow. Bring it back to me and I will give you what you want." She leaves and begins to knock on her neighbor's doors and like her Christian counterpart hears the same things.

The difference in the two stories is in the ending – the moral, if you will – the meaning of the story for the tellers and the listeners.

The Christian woman never returns to the religious leader. She gets caught up in sharing and easing the sorrows of others and her own pain is lessened as she ministers to the world.

The Buddhist woman returns to her brother, tells him that she has learned that all life is made up of suffering, asks to be allowed to retreat from life, and becomes the first Buddhist nun.

Theologically, each story reflects the beliefs of its religion. The stories are not interchangeable: Christians cannot learn Christian faith from the Buddhist story and Buddhists cannot learn Buddhist tenets from the Christian story. Both are good stories – but they only teach a moral in their own context.

A moral isn't a necessary element of non-religious stories but it is necessary for Christian storytellers in Christian venues. Given the power of stories that we have been talking about for so much of this book, the moral of a Christian story is vital.

Make sure that your story told in Christian venues is a good story, make sure it matters - and make sure that the point of it, the moral of it, fits with our theology and the tenets of our faith.

Questions –

1. Can you think of a story that has more than one ending? How would you chose which one to use? Give an example.

2. Do you think morals need to be explicit or could they be implicit? Can people figure out the point of a story on their own or should the storyteller make it clear?

3. Are there any tenets of our faith that are inappropriate for storytelling? Why? Give an example.

Elements of Storytelling

Storytelling has three basic elements: the voice, the body, and the emotions.

Chapter 12: Voice

Storytellers use sounds, words, inflections and tone to convey a story and its meaning.

Elderly, slightly eccentric, sometimes confused, Roy was one of those "pillars of the church", and he loved to help lead worship. So the worship chair scheduled him to be the liturgist as often as she could and especially on special Sundays. One Easter morning, Roy was scheduled to read.

I was, as always at that church, uneasy with the laity reading the gospel. After all, I was seminary trained, a life-long reader, and good at reading aloud. But I sat waiting with my usual smile as Roy fumbled for the page and muttered to himself.

And then he began to read the account in John of Mary Magdalene's encounter with the gardener, the risen Jesus. When he got to the part where Jesus said Mary's name, Roy read it with all the emotion that it must have had when Jesus said it: disbelief that she didn't know him, love for her and the expectation of love in return, and power enough to jolt her from her anguish. Power enough to make me sit up and notice too. "Mary!" It was the best reading of the Easter scriptures that I've ever heard.

Sometimes there is just one word that conveys a whole story – say it right and we'll understand all the things you don't say.

Questions –

1. Record your voice and listen to it. Is your voice well-suited to storytelling? What do you like about it or dislike about it?

2. Can you project well? Enunciate well? Emote well? How can you learn to do each one better?

3. Do you know how to fluctuate the tone of your voice? Can you raise and lower it as the story demands? What might you need to practice in order to do what Roy did with the word "Mary?"

Chapter 13: Body

Storytellers use gestures, facial expressions, movements, and body language to convey a story and its meaning.

I don't remember the girl's name. She was one of many girls in one of many UMYF groups in one of many churches I've served. But I do remember that she was deaf, read lips, and spoke with only a slight distortion.

We were practicing interviewing techniques as some of the youth were getting ready to look for summer jobs. And I was playing the role of a prospective employer.

The youth had filled out their "application forms" and were coming in my "office" one by one. As each one came in, I smiled in welcome, introduced myself, invited them to sit, and began asking them typical interview questions, still smiling as I tried to put them at ease.

It went well until this girl came in the room. She looked surprised and confused; she stumbled over words much more than usual. She couldn't answer my questions and seemed to have forgotten the whole purpose of the exercise.

Someone who spoke ASL talked with her and learned the problem. She was confused by my smile. It didn't match my words. There was nothing in an interview, in the introduction or the questions that was funny, pleasant, or otherwise deserving of a smile. It was a difficult situation and rather than making her feel welcome and at ease, the smile was disconcerting because it didn't match.

Sometimes it isn't just what you say or even how you say it. Sometimes your body language, gestures, facial movements can add to – or detract from – your meaning.

Questions –

1. Record yourself during a sermon or other storytelling event. Watch it with the sound off. Do your movements fit the space you are in? Match the movement of the story? Enhance the point you want the story to make?

2. If someone heard your story who didn't understand your language, what would they learn from your face and gestures?

3. How can you become more comfortable with your body and its gestures and movements?

Chapter 14: Heart

Storytellers use emotion to convey a story and its meaning.

Princeton Theological Seminary intends its graduates to be good preachers. When I was a student there, first year students were required to take two semesters of speech class; second year students, two semesters of preaching class; and after that, we could chose from elective courses.

My second semester speech professor was away one week and her husband, also a speech professor, filled in for her. Our assignment was to read a psalm aloud in class. I was a typical first year seminary student who had learned to read scripture by imitating the elderly men of my childhood churches.

So I stood behind the lectern and in my best "preacher voice" intoned the words of Psalm 46... "God is our refuge and strength, a very present help in trouble. Therefore will not we fear, though the earth be removed, and though the mountains be carried into the midst of the sea..."

The substitute professor stopped me, pulled a stool close to the lectern, leaned into my personal space, and said, "My wife and I just split up. Tell me some words of comfort..."

Before I even processed that he wasn't being literal, my emotions poured out those words in a very different way... "God is our refuge and strength, a very present help in trouble!"

In that second reading, I may not have said the words in perfect King James English, but I got the emotions right. The rest of the class knew that Psalm's story of mercy and protection when the last word was read.

Questions –

1. Do you find it easy or difficult to be emotionally available in the pulpit? Do you find public displays of emotion embarrassing or enlightening? How will your own emotions affect the ways in which you tell stories?

2. Is it okay to chose not to tell emotional stories or read scripture emotionally if you aren't comfortable with that? Why or why not?

3. Think of an emotionally charge section of scripture. Who in your congregation might be touched by an emotionally open reading of it? How might that impact your relationship with them after the scripture is read?

Uses of Storytelling

Stories enable us to accomplish our daily work so that we can accomplish the bigger task of telling the story of God in the world through Christ.

Chapter 15: Worship

Storytellers use stories in worship structure; in sermons; in the offering, prayers and sacraments; and in children's moments.

Worship Structure

Storytellers use stories as the basis for the structure of worship.

My first semester of a Doctor of Ministry program included a class on using stories in worship. I decided to put together a way of organizing worship that in itself told a story.

Now the lectionary does this so if you are using that to plan your preaching, you are already in the framework of God's relationship with humanity through time, particularly through Jesus' birth, life, death, and resurrection.

But I wanted to focus this on a short period – a summer series of worship services – and I wanted to go off the lectionary for a those weeks. I started with Genesis, ended with Revelation, and covered the high places of Christian faith in between. I also wanted each worship service to tell a story so I designed a format for the services that included setting, characters, and plot.

My theory was that by creating those frameworks, people would be taken inside the scriptural story, would connect to the scripture, and connect to God as a preparation for hearing a sermon that could then bring them even further into the relationship.

I tried the theory out on my congregation over the next summer and it did work. Even if they didn't consciously recognize the story framework, they felt the flow of the services each Sunday and across the Sundays of the summer. They were receptive to the stories in the sermon because those stories were all located within the larger story.

By the way, I got an A on the paper!

Questions –

1. Can you think of a plot that you would like to retell during a season of the church year? Outline what that would look like in one service and across the series of services.

2. Can you think of a character or series of characters you would like to tell about during a service or though a series of services? Outline what that would look like.

3. Can you think of a setting or a series of settings that could uphold a story or series of stories told in one service or series of services? For example, could you format a service around the setting of a garden? A grave? A sheepfold?

Sermons

Storytellers use stories in sermons to illuminate their points and to connect people to scripture, to each other, and to God.

In seminary, I took a class on narrative preaching. My sermon topic was the relationship between Sarah, Abraham, and Hagar and the form was first person narrative. I began speaking from Sarah's perspective, then became Abraham, and finished as Hagar.

I was terrified and no matter what the professor said, I refused to set aside my written sermon. Part way through Sarah, sitting in a rocking chair on one side of the stage, the papers slid from my lap and scattered across the floor!

Looking at the video tape later, I was horrified as well as terrified! With the ten pounds extra the camera adds – as well as the "freshmen fifteen" – I looked as big as Abraham's tent! And with papers all over the floor, I looked about as coordinated as one of his camels.

It was a humbling moment. And it took some time before I could look beyond those things to see whether or not the story could have worked had I been a better storyteller.

Storytelling, as I've been insisting from the beginning of this book, is not child's play. Storytelling is serious stuff – it has great power – and it takes significant work. Using stories in worship is absolutely fitting but be prepared to put in the time necessary to be fully prepared for the telling.

Realize that you won't be the best storyteller in your first tale told but be willing to lay down your papers and put yourself out there. Here are a few ideas for how to use stories in worship and the sermon:

- Place a story within your sermon to highlight a point. These stories can come from many sources.
  o personal experiences
  o church history and traditions
  o folk tales, books, or movies
- Use the sermon to retell a scripture story or to weave a story around a section of scripture that isn't narrative.
- Write the whole sermon as a story.

And remember to put away the papers when the time comes to tell it!

NOTE:

I want to add a word here about jokes as some preachers think they are good ice breakers.

My sister told me a joke once: String walked into a bar and sat down on a stool. "Give me a drink!" The bartender said, "We don't serve String." String got down from the stool, dejected, and walked down the street to the next bar. The same conversation ensued. And again and again and again.

Finally, String came out of the bar, threw himself down on the sidewalk, tossed himself against a lamp pole, beat himself on a wall, and finally fell in a pile on the sidewalk. Then he picked himself up and walked into the last bar.

"Give me a drink!" "We don't serve String!" "I'm Knot!"

Now, I don't remember why that joke seemed so funny to me but I do remember cleaning it up (restaurants instead of bars) and adding it to several sermons. I don't think it offended anyone, I don't think it belittled anyone, I don't think it made fun of anyone. But also, looking back, I'm not sure it got across what was probably my point about the relationship of God and a battered humanity.

Be very careful if you use jokes at all that they don't harm and do help the intention of your sermon.

Questions –

1. Can you list the ways in which you would like to use stories in your sermons? Schedule those stories now so you have plenty of time to prepare.

2. Do you know a joke that doesn't have any negatives and does have a positive point? Would you tell it in a sermon? Do jokes have a place in preaching?

3. Have you ever shared a story from a first-person perspective? How would you prepare to do that?

The Offering, Sacraments, Prayer

Storytellers use stories to enlarge a congregation's experience of various elements in the worship service.

My father-in-law is also a pastor. He has a unique ministry with people who have had difficulty in their lives. They often don't have much to put in the offering plate on Sundays but they put in whatever they have with a grateful heart.

His congregation repeats a proclamation at the offering – they even have it printed on laminated cards for visitors and new members – that places their offering firmly within the story of their lives and God's salvation. "I have never been without... God has always brought me out."

One congregation I served had a fall stewardship campaign where individuals got up each Sunday for several weeks to talk about the different ministries of the church and how the offering helped. It was the story of the church's relationship to God. The congregation was the setting, the individuals were the characters, and their money was the plot that moved the church toward God's calling.

However your congregations handle the offering, never forget that it is part of the story of their relationship to God and to each other. Take the offering out of that story and the money becomes nothing more than an obligation.

Other elements of worship are intrinsically story-oriented, as well. The sacraments are stories – stories of experiences in scripture translated through stories of the early church into the stories of our lives and our relationship with God.

The prayers of the people are stories – the joys and concerns of the stories of their lives. The call to worship is the "once upon a time" and the benediction is the "happily ever after." Music tells stories in the lines of the songs and those songs have a back story to tell: the story of the author's experiences that led to that hymn, chorus, etc.

At every part of the worship service you can pause, share a story of your own, and listen to the ways these actions meet up with the stories of your congregation's lives and faith. It can be a powerful time for all of you.

Questions –

1. Do you know a story to go with the offering? The call to worship? Prayer time? How would you use those stories in those parts of worship?

2. How often can you tell the same stories? What would happen if you told the same story each week at the offering?

3. How many stories are appropriate in one worship service? Should you have a schedule for storytelling or should it be spontaneous? Are there people who would dislike too many stories? Why or why not?

Children's Moments

Storytellers use stories to include children in worship and to make worship accessible to children.

I've left this topic till last in this chapter about worship – because it is the first place some people think about telling stories. And, yes, do tell stories in the children's moments. Tell good stories that create a feeling but don't dwell on morals and points – especially with young children who can't absorb them.

But there are other ways to tell stories with the children and youth in your congregation.

This year, I was reading the Palm Sunday scripture from Matthew, which mentions the children in the Temple shouting "Hosanna!" I had the children lead us in the praise and prayer opening of worship that day and connected our children to the children in the scripture story. It made the scripture children come alive to me and it made the children with me that Sunday visible as the prophetic voices they can be.

Several years ago, I made communion bread with the children during Sunday School before worship. I remember one little girl taking the bread out of the oven so carefully and carrying it into the sanctuary so reverently. She helped serve the bread to the congregation and she held it as the body of Christ in her hands. Without words she was telling a story of faith to the adults around her.

Many times, I've had a group of children act out the scripture – no preparation ahead of time, just me reading the scripture and them doing what I read. In one congregation, a group of youth performed skits that we rehearsed each week. Once I drew out a scripture setting on the floor, complete with ribbon river and plastic snakes, and the children walked the plot with me as I read the story. In another congregation, the lay readers were always children, standing on a box behind the pulpit when they were too small to be seen.

Teenage acolytes enact the story of Christ entering into worship with us, and going into the world ahead of us at the end of worship.

Even prayer time can be a special time for the children and youth to experience God's presence in the stories of our lives. In a children's Bible study, the students were telling me all the reasons they didn't like worship. One girl, about ten, said, "Except for prayer. Don't change prayer. It's the only time we talk about the things that really matter."

In short, there are unlimited ways for you to help children experience worship through stories. Don't limit yourself in exploring them.

Questions –

1. Have you ever told a story to a child? What was the setting and how did it turn out? How can you be better prepared the next time?

2. Have you ever asked a child to tell you a story? What was different about it than the way you would have told it? If you haven't ever done this, do it this week. Then look at whether there's a lesson for you in there.

3. When you plan a children's story is it for the sake of the children or the adults who are listening? Who is more important at that time? How do you balance keeping the adults interested while ministering to the children?

Chapter 16: Spiritual Direction

Storytellers recognize and share the spiritual life as a story.

When I was nineteen I had a vision. I was in a difficult time in my life: exhausted, frightened, and lonely. I went to bed one night and prayed, "God, if you really exist, if you really care for me, prove it."

As I lay there staring at the dark ceiling, I noticed a light shining in the corner. There were two windows in the room but light from them didn't reflect in that corner and so I began watching it more closely, trying to figure out what it was.

It looked like a star but it was moving – I realized it was coming closer from a long way off. As it grew larger, I could see that it vibrated and pulsated. And then it came so close that I could see that it was a large white bird, a dove.

It soared around my bedroom, circling above me, and I was absolutely terrified that it would touch me. I cried out, with the words of disciples and prophets, "Don't! I'm not good enough!" And eventually, the dove sailed away as it had come.

I wish I could tell you that story and say that it was the end of all my lonely nights, that I heard that call from God clearly and entered the ministry the next day, that I understood what happened in any way beyond the most basic. But I can't tell you that.

All I can say is that after that night I never wondered if God existed or if God cared for me. It took me many years to come to any closer relationship with God or understanding of God. And I was many years into ministry before I realized that that vision was my first calling.

What I come back to time and again as I think about that vision is that I had no faith community in which to explore its meaning. I didn't attend church any longer but, more importantly, I couldn't even imagine a conversation about this with the people – clergy or laity - in any of the churches I had once attended.

How different my life might have been if someone had encouraged me to tell my spiritual story! God and I are the main characters in that story, but we shouldn't have been the only characters. There should have been a community to hear it; unfortunately, I didn't know that at the time.

You have a congregation full of people who have a spiritual story – it might be a vision or a dark night of the soul or a long quiet friendship. Like me at nineteen, they may not understand all the ways in which God is moving through their lives. You can help them to recognize their spiritual story by telling your own, by asking questions, and by showing that it is safe to talk about such things.

Questions –

1. Are you or have you ever participated in formal Spiritual Direction? What was that experience like? Do you feel comfortable guiding a congregation spiritually?

2. Can you tell your own spiritual stories? Have you ever done so? How did it feel and what impact did it have on you?

3. Have you ever asked individuals to tell you their spiritual stories? How did they respond? If it wasn't a positive experience, how can you prepare so that the next time it will be?

Chapter 17: Education

Storytellers use stories in all aspects of Christian Education: Sunday School, Bible Study, Vacation Bible School, etc.

There is a Sufi folktale called *The Ancient Coffer of Nuri Bey.* It's the story of a wealthy older businessman who marries a much younger woman. He comes home from a trip to find the household in a turmoil. The wife has locked herself in her room with a wooden box – "large enough to hold a man" - that used to hold his mother's embroidery. She wouldn't allow her husband's oldest servant to look inside. She gave her husband the key but suggested that if he trusted her he wouldn't need to open the box. He agreed, called two other servants, had them carry the box to the furthest corner of the property, and bury it. Nuri Bey and his wife never spoke of it again.

I've told this story so many times over the years, it feels like Nuri Bey, his wife, and I are old friends! The lonely wife, the jealous servant, the shrewd husband... I know them all, the looks they give each other, the harbored resentments, the silence throughout the years.

But even so, I still get a little shock each time I read it or retell it – the burying of a secret with such finality.

I've also found that it does that to others who hear it. Students never agree about what is in that coffer, that box that is buried. Some think it is nothing but embroidery, others that it's a man – or a baby. Some even think it is jewels or treasure.

Once students have begun to open their minds to the many things that could be in the coffer – once they've heard each other and thought through the reasoning behind those answers – once they've realized that we'll never know for sure! – then they can begin to think through the societal parts of the story. What is the relationship between this husband and wife? Where do the servants fit in? Or the mother? What societal beliefs about the role of men and women come into play here?

And ultimately, after all of that, students can get to the mystical heart of the Sufi story: what are our religious beliefs about the relationship of humanity to God?

As Christian teachers, we don't need to look to Sufi stories for our teaching – there are plenty of stories in scripture. But they are so familiar to us that we aren't shocked by them any more, we don't need to discuss answers to the questions we no longer hear, we aren't forced back into the story to get a fuller understanding.

Too often we go right to the last question - what does this say about God – and take the pat answer to the question that our students have heard and repeated so often. We fail to take them deeper into their understanding of God, of ourselves, and of the relationship between us all.

Good storytelling can change that. Allow your telling of the scriptural stories to explore all their power to shock, to open student's minds to new ideas and thoughts, to lead us gradually from the story through the culture and into new territory in our relationship with God.

Questions –

1. What is the most shocking story you've ever told? Did it have a point that could have been made without the shock?

2. Do you ever find yourself bored by reading a section of scripture over and over again? How might storytelling bring it alive for you again?

3. Take a section of scripture that you think you know well – the details and the meaning – and have a good storyteller read it aloud to you. Did you see a new layer of meaning?

Chapter 18: Pastoral Care

Storytellers use stories in counseling, at weddings and funerals – in all those situations where they are called to caring relationships with others.

A half dozen years ago, a good friend died. He had been pastor, mentor, and challenging friend for many years. At his funeral, his family put together a booklet full of pictures of him and pieces he had written. It was the story of his life and, better than any words any of us said at the funeral, it told of the fullness and richness of his life story. Seeing that booklet helped me cope with the loss of this good friend.

A decade or so before that, I held my first *Holiday Tea* in a small country church. One weekday afternoon in early November, I invited all the women who had lost their husbands during the previous year. The topic was simply how they were going to handle the holidays alone. I had books and pamphlets laying on the table, and a pot of hot water on the stove and a few cookies on a plate.

But I had no prepared script. These women had been through a situation that I had never faced: the death of a spouse. What could I say to them that they couldn't say better? What I could do however, was listen to their stories. And so I simply asked, "What has it been like?" and they flooded me with answers.

The women sat around my table all afternoon, talking about what they missed about their husbands, and their fears about facing the upcoming holidays. They gave each other suggestions, they voiced ideas they hadn't known they had, and their mutual stories helped them cope.

Sometime between those two experiences, I received a phone call from a nun who had been given my name by a mutual friend.

The nun and her three sisters had an elderly mother who needed to sell her home. The mother refused and the four sisters disagreed about what should happen next. Everyone was angry with each other and they needed outside help.

The nun asked me to intermediate a conversation between the four sisters that would lead to them making a united decision that would help their mother face the last years of her life.

We met in the nun's apartment and sat in her dark but cozy living room. I began by telling them a little about myself and then had them share their life story with me and with each other. Each one talked uninterruptedly for five minutes or more about their relationship with their parents and about their lives today. As they went around the room, each sister heard things about her siblings that she hadn't heard (or hadn't absorbed) before.

As they talked, each heard bits of her own story in the story of the others: common ground in the midst of their differences. And as they shared more about this common ground, they formed new hopes and dreams for their future and their mother's.

When the meeting was over, they went as a group to their mother's house, shared with her some of the stories they had told each other, shared how much they loved her, shared their common concern for her. That sharing enabled her to cope with a decision about her home based on their love rather than on fear or anger.

Pastoral care is difficult work – whether we are counseling others or getting through our own difficulties. Sometimes, the most helpful thing can be to simply tell our story or listen to others tell theirs. Use your stories to give people space to open up their minds and hearts, to truly listen to those around them, and to understand the value of their own human story as well.

Questions –

1. On your next pastoral visit, look at a photograph or object in the room and ask the parishioner about it. Later reflect on these questions: did they tell you facts or a story? Did they talk about the object or the emotions attached to it? Did they reflect on that one object or on the whole of their lives?

2. Role-play a counseling situation in which stories are used to get at the heart of a situation. How did the stories support or strain the relationship?

3. Think of a story that has helped you through a difficult time. What about it strengthened you? Was it setting, character, plot, or moral?

Chapter 19: Evangelism

Storytellers use stories to tell seekers about Christ.

A few years ago, I attended a continuing education event at Princeton Theological Seminary. The topic was Emerging Worship and the speakers included a woman who was the pastor of an emerging congregation.

Her congregation was mostly made up of young adults, some with families, who were new to Christian faith. Many of these young adults had not been brought up in a church, didn't know the Bible or its stories, and didn't know the basic tenets of Christianity. She was frank with them at the start of each worship service that she understood that they were not there because they had faith but that she believed that if they listened to what she had to say about Jesus they would come to that place.

As she taught them about Jesus, they liked what they learned and they tried to incorporate those things into their lives. This pastor instituted a time of testimony into the worship service, meeting with those who wanted to speak then and helping them prepare for how they would give their testimony.

She shared with us in that one of those speakers had made a strong impression on her. He stood up before the congregation and said that he lied at work. His boss knew it and expected it; in many ways his job depended on his being willing to lie the way the boss wanted him to lie.

But he said, tears in his eyes, as he was learning more about Jesus, he realized that he couldn't continue to lie at work any more. That even if it meant losing his job, he had to be true to the way that Jesus was teaching him to live.

The pastor said that story also had a tremendous impact on the not-yet Christians in the congregation. If this man thought Jesus was worth losing his job for, maybe they should know more about Jesus themselves.

There are hundreds of church growth books available – I have dozens on my bookshelves as you probably have or will have over the years. But I can say without any hesitancy, that the greatest tool for evangelism is simply telling the story of how Jesus has changed your life.

If all laity and clergy were able to tell one story like that young man's story about his job, we would have full sanctuaries every Sunday. Whether it's testimony given in worship, or to a stranger on a bus, or a new friend at the grocery store, or any of a hundred other places, those stories will attract others who will want a similar story in their own lives.

Questions –

1. Can you tell a story about how Jesus changed you? How old is the story? Can you think of a story from yesterday or last week?

2. Are there opportunities in your regular worship setting for telling personal faith stories? What is that like? How do people respond to it?

3. When was the last time you had a conversation with a non-Christian about your faith? Did you talk about facts and tenets of faith or did you tell your own faith story? Would the conversation have been different with a story?

Chapter 20: Administration

Storytellers use stories in meetings, vision planning, goal setting, and conflict resolution.

There are three administration stories I want to tell you – all are interrelated and come from the same congregation.

I became their pastor after their former pastor retired. She had had a long ministry there but there was a good deal of conflict in the last few years. Some of that related to a situation that had ended with the exodus of several families to a neighboring church.

To the extent that I have been able to figure it out, from the varying stories told, this is what happened: a small group in the church had decided the building needed to be made handicap accessible. This group raised funds regularly and then used those funds to purchase items for the church without going through any official church body. If they saw the need for new kitchen utensils, for example, they bought them.

There had been small problems: a purchase that had resulted in grievances with the sexton, etc. But on the whole the congregation accepted that these women – leaders in many other ways – would provide the extras that the church needed.

So they investigated buying a chair lift for the church. They began raising money and making decisions and assumed they had permission to do so, based on years of similar actions.

When the pastor and administrative board began saying that an elevator would be a better idea, they felt frustrated, angry, and betrayed.

Much of the pastoral care I did in my first year there was to listen over and over to the story of this event from the perspective of the remaining members of the now-defunct small group and the administrative leaders.

As I listened to their stories, I never entered an opinion, just listened to the heartfelt truth they each told. But I also began to work administratively to prevent such problems in the future. I tried to make sure that everyone knew that all ideas were welcomed; that opposing viewpoints were okay; that not all votes had to be unanimous but that if there were great divisions, a decision couldn't be reached. I tried to model the premise that, if we disagreed on something, we did so as Christians, still loving each other after the disagreement.

I also looked for those stories that would tie the opposing sides together. I found one in the story of a homebound woman who had been a long-time member of the congregation. She said to me one day, on the subject of the building's continued inaccessibility, "My daughter told me I'm on the 'shut-in' list at the church. But I'm not a 'shut-in' – I'm a 'shut-out!' I can get to the doctor's, to the bank, to the grocery store – everywhere except my own church and I'm shut out there."

As we discussed accessibility over the next few years, I told her story often. People began to see that the question wasn't which side won the argument but how the two sides could come together so that no other person was shut out from the life of the church.

As we began preparation to rebuild the back entrance to the church so that accessibility could happen, someone found a large earthenware jug. On a recommendation in a book by Kent Ira Groff, I had it brought to an administrative meeting and set in the middle of the table.

I asked if anyone knew what it was and where it came from. The oldest members of the council remembered it immediately - an old man in the congregation has used it to make lemonade for picnics in their youth! They told the stories about him and the picnics and their memories of those days. They brought the past into the present and we used that to build on for the future: this congregation that had been here for so long would continue on and the older folk would continue to be productive members as the building was more accessible to them.

There might have been a shorter way to get to agreement on the accessibility issue. But the sharing of these stories built community around a difficult subject and allowed the administrative leadership to do their job in that community. I think it was worth the wait.

Questions –

1. Do you know the story of the congregation where you are currently serving or worshipping? If not, how could you learn it? If so, how could you retell it?

2. Learn the story of one founder of the congregation and tell it to someone not involved with that church in any way. What impact did the story have on that person?

3. Think about the current leadership of the congregation, particularly any who are difficult to work with. Have you heard their life story? Do you know the story of their experiences in the church? Could hearing those stories help the relationships? Is there any way it could be detrimental? How can you prepare for the unknowns of this process?

Praxis of Storytelling

Storytelling takes preparation, practice, and presentation.

Chapter 21:
A method for learning to tell a story.

There are many tried and true methods for learning and telling stories. Here is my rendition of those methods.

1. Read many stories. Pray. (Consider prayer to be part of all the following.)
2. Read them again. And again. And again.
3. Chose stories you like, that feel right to you, that make a point you'd want to live by, that match the faith you proclaim, that lead and guide you to a closer relationship with God and better understanding of the message of Christ.
4. Pick one of those stories that suits the occasion on which you will tell it.
5. Read it aloud to someone else and listen to the thoughts and feelings they get from the story.
6. Paraphrase the story – tell it aloud in your own words.
7. Tell the story aloud from the perspective of the main character.
8. Tell the story aloud from the perspective of any other character.
9. Enter into the sensory world of the story and answer the following questions:
     a. What do you see?
     b. What do you hear?
     c. What do you taste?
     d. What do you smell?
     e. What do you feel?
10. Draw a series of pictures of the story. These can be detailed story boards or simple stick figure drawings. Just so long as you can see in front of you the setting, the characters, and the plot.
11. Assume the identity of any character in the story and let someone else interview you. Maintain that character's identity throughout the interview even if you are distracted or interrupted.

12. When you have become fully a part of the story then prepare how you will tell it.
13. If you are going to read it, will it be from a sheet of paper, or from a book? Which form will help your audience absorb the story?
14. If you are going to tell it from memory, what helps might you need? A note card? An outline? An object? Will you be the only one to see it or will the congregation see it too?
15. If you are going to act it out, where will you move, how will you dress, how will you transition into and out of character?
16. After you've made these choices and prepared for them, practice. Practice alone, practice in front of a mirror, and then practice with an audience.
17. Tell your finished story to at least one of the people you read it to at first. Get their feedback and decide if you need to make any final edits.
18. Continue praying, and tell your story.

Chapter 22:
A list of hints for storytellers.

Learn your story, get to know it, prepare to tell it, and then share it. Here are some hints to help you.

1. Learn
   a. Learn about your audience as well as your story.
   b. Chose appropriate stories and appropriate language levels.

2. Know
   a. Internalize rather than memorize the story.
   b. See it in your mind
   c. Become friends with your characters.
   d. Remember characters have feelings. So does your audience.
   e. Be sure of the perspective of the storyteller: will you be a participant or an observer?

3. Prepare
   a. Is this an attention-arresting story (short, staccato) or a still-life story (meandering, leisurely)?
   b. Plan for repetition not redundancy
   c. Hear the rhythms and inflections within the story and try to match them with your voice.
   d. Use active words, not forms of "to be".
   e. Be consistent.
   f. Use direct conversation where possible – dialog rather than narration.
   g. Make an emotional appeal; use suspense to draw people in.
   h. Get rid of "that," "which," "who" and other unnecessary words.
   i. Look at sentence length and structure: are they appropriate for the story and the audience?

4. Share
   a. Avoid distracting jewelry or clothing.
   b. Tell one point per story!
   c. Give all and only necessary information.
   d. Wrap things up.
   e. Use pauses effectively.
   f. Use correct grammar ("says" not "goes").
   g. Match your gestures to the story and to the space you are in.
   h. Get listener participation if possible.
   i. Be natural and comfortable
   j. Don't be "iffy" – or a "reluctant starter". Don't sabotage your story with indecision.
   k. Appeal to the audience's senses and imagination
   l. Tell each story fresh each time.
   m. Enjoy the story!

Conclusion

Who are you to tell stories to others?

Like me, you are people with stories. They might be stories you grew up with or learned in seminary. They might be stories you've read or heard or thought or written. They are, hopefully, stories that have impacted your life, changed you, molded you into the people you are or hope to be.

You have every right to tell those stories.

You also have an obligation to tell some of those stories. The ones that will impact someone else's life, change their hearts or minds - the ones that might help them become the people God wants them to be.

Hopefully, this book has given you some insights into how to do that.

It won't, however, make you into a good storyteller. Only you can do that. Tell your stories. Tell them often. Tell them with love and compassion.

That will make you a good storyteller, fit company for the One who is the model for all our storytelling, the Ultimate Storyteller of the Ultimate Story.

NOTES

www.ingramcontent.com/pod-product-compliance
Lightning Source LLC
Chambersburg PA
CBHW030944090426
42737CB00007B/535